NATURE CURE FOR
ASTHMA AND HAY FEV

Immediate relief from the distressing symptoms is naturally the sufferer's main concern during an attack of asthma or hay fever, but more important is the need to remove the *root causes*. Nature Cure treatment is based on this need, and this book offers real and lasting health in place of the constant fear of a recurrence which clouds the lives of those who rely only on orthodox medical treatment.

Nature Cure for Asthma and Hay Fever

Alan Moyle N.D., M.B.N.O.A.

THORSONS PUBLISHERS LIMITED
Wellingborough, Northamptonshire

First published 1951
Eighth Impression 1972
Second Edition, revised and reset, 1975
Second Impression 1976
Third Impression 1978

ISBN 0 7225 0294 X

Typeset by Specialised Offset Services Ltd., Liverpool
and printed and bound by Weatherby Woolnough
Wellingborough, Northamptonshire

Contents

I.
Asthma and Hay Fever

Asthma and hay fever are grouped together in what are regarded as anaphylactic phenomena. That is to say, they are conditions of excessive sensitiveness exhibited by certain individuals when injected with anti-toxin serum or exposed to the emanation of various animals (horses, cats, fowls), or in the vicinity of certain plants, etc. A more accurate definition, of course, is allergy, for the symptoms demonstrated in asthma and hay fever are allergic in character. Allergy implies a special sensitiveness of a person to certain foods, animals emanations, insect bites, pollens or other products of plants.

Asthma and hay fever are respiratory diseases influenced by an allergic condition. Asthma ('I gasp for breath') is a disorder of respiration manifested by paroxysms of difficult breathing. Hay fever is an inflammatory condition of the mucous membranes of the eyes, nose and air passages which usually arises during the period from May to July, when haymaking is in progress.

To appreciate fully the causes of asthma and hay fever, the changes that arise as a result of these diseases, and the cure, it is necessary to have some knowledge of the mechanism of respiration and of what allergy means. It is proposed, therefore, to discuss the anatomy and physiology of the lungs and respiratory function and the question of allergy before proceeding further.

BREATHING
Breathing, or respiration, is of course the process by which

air passes into (inspiration) and out of (expiration) the lungs, and it is in this way that the body is provided with life-giving oxygen, and expels the products of oxidation, such as carbon dioxide and other poisonous gases. It is this oxidization of absorbed materials which provides the cells with energy.

The air passages are composed of the nose, throat, larynx, trachea (or windpipe) and the bronchial tubes. On breathing in, air is drawn through the nasal passages. It is extremely important to breathe through the nose, because while the inspired air is passing through the nasal passages it is warmed and made relatively free from dust and particles. The small hairs lining the sides of the nose assist the filtering of the air, and at the top and back of the nostrils are three passages, in which the air is warmed, moistened and cleaned.

In the pharynx the food and air passages meet. Nature, however, provides a very clever arrangement — the epiglottis — which covers the larynx during the act of swallowing and prevents solids or liquid matter from entering the larynx. The larynx, therefore, is open at all times except when food or drink is actually being swallowed. The larynx, incidentally, contains the vocal cords, and it is by the vibration of these that sounds and voice are produced.

The inspired air continues from the larynx into the trachea. The trachea, commonly called the windpipe, is about 10 to 11 centimetres long. It is a cartilaginous and membranous tube. There are 16 to 20 rings made of cartilage, bound together by muscle in the formation of the trachea. By this arrangement the trachea becomes an elastic tube which, while yielding with the turning and bending of the neck, still permits a free passage of air to the lungs. The trachea, like the nose and larynx, is lined with mucous membrane.

The trachea subdivides into right and left bronchi. The right bronchus is wider, shorter and more vertical than the left. The bronchi are similar in structure to the trachea and possess the same mucous membrane. Each of the bronchi subdivides into smaller and smaller tubes which are called bronchioles. The larger bronchioles are composed of fibrous tissue, smooth circular muscular fibres, and internally mucous membrane. The bronchioles penetrate every part of the lungs and end in groups of air-cells called alveoli.

The mucous membrane lining the trachea and bronchi demonstrates what is known as *columnar ciliated cells*. The function of the cilia is to pass backwards, towards the mouth, any foreign matter that has been inhaled. The movement is by very quick, firm strokes. During inflammations, when quantities of phlegm are being discharged from the mucous membrane, this ciliary movement ensures the passage of phlegm to the larynx, where it can be expelled or swallowed. In this way the air passages are kept free. Mucous membrane is looser and lighter than true skin, which it resembles, but it is lubricated by mucus which is secreted from small mucus glands under the membrane. Mucous membrane is a delicate lining, though it displays great pliability.

THE LUNGS

The lungs are two spongy, elastic organs which practically occupy the whole of the chest. Each lung is almost conical in shape, the base resting on the diaphragm, the apex of each lung projecting into the neck. The outer, rounded surface of each lung is in contact with the adjacent ribs. The heart lies in between the lungs, and there is a connection by way of the pulmonary arteries, which carry deoxygenated – impure – blood to the lungs from the right ventricle of the heart, and by the pulmonary veins, which carry oxygenated – pure – blood to the left auricle of the heart. In this instance the pulmonary arteries carry venous blood and the pulmonary veins arterial or pure blood, this being opposite to the normal description applied to the blood-stream. Note also that the heart, lying between the lungs, must be affected by changes in volume of the lungs.

Each lung is enveloped in a membrane called the pleura. This is constructed in such a way that one layer of the membrane is adherent to the lung and the other layer to the inner surface of one half of the chest, the two layers forming the pleural cavity. Thus there is a pleural cavity each side of the chest.

The lungs are, of course, protected by the spine and ribs at the back and by the ribs and their costal cartilages and sternum at the sides and front. This is called the thorax or chest, and is designed not only for normal protection but also for mobility. The thorax is highly expansile in structure to allow for the changes in volume of the lungs.

The structure of each lung is the same, except that the right lung possesses three lobes and the left only two. There is the main bronchus, which subdivides into bronchioles and continues this subdivision until the capillary bronchi are only one hundredth of an inch in diameter. The smallest divisions of the bronchial tubes open into a number of dilations which are covered with alveoli. Each alveolus consists of a delicate membrane strengthened by elastic fibres, and it is these alveoli that supply the elasticity of the lungs.

Branches of the pulmonary artery accompany the bronchial tubes and, like the bronchi, subdivide again and again. In this way delicate capillaries come to lie in between the alveoli, so that air and blood are separated only by two delicate membranes. By a process of diffusion an interchange of gases takes place. The pure blood is collected by the network of capillaries belonging to the pulmonary veins, which take it to the heart, there to be pumped all over the body. The living tissue is itself nourished by another and smaller set of blood-vessels.

This interchange takes place between the fine blood capillaries and tissue cells via the tissue fluid. The oxygen is derived from the oxygenated blood, and as the blood loses its oxygen and takes up carbon dioxide it is transferred back to the lungs by the venous system. This intricate system of blood-supply covers the whole of the body.

THE VITAL ELEMENT

Life could not be maintained for more than a short time without oxygen. This vital element is a source of heat and provides the energy for all cellular activity. The table below gives the difference between inspired air and expired air:

	Inspired Air	Expired Air
Oxygen	20.96	16.4
Nitrogen	79.00	79.5
Carbon dioxide	0.04	4.1

A person could not live in a sealed room long before a state of asphyxia would arise, because the carbon dioxide content of the air would steadily rise and the oxygen content decrease. If the carbon dioxide rose to 6 per cent, together with oxygen starvation, death would speedily follow.

Asphyxiation develops in three stages: increase of rate and depth of breathing (in an effort to overcome the oxygen shortage); expiratory convulsions; and slow, deep inspirations combined with increasing exhaustion.

The normal respiration rate varies according to age, sex, exercise, etc. The usual rates per minute are: baby, 30; child, 26; adult, 16. The heart/respiration rate is about 4.5 to 1. After exercise both the heart and lungs work faster, but the ratio should be fairly constant.

At any time there is always a certain amount of air in the lungs; this is called *stationary* air. By a prolonged outward breath about half of the stationary air can be expelled. The air which passes in and out of the lungs in ordinary normal breathing is termed *tidal* air. The *vital capacity* is the amount of air that can be forcibly expelled after the deepest possible breath. It varies with posture and disease but is of diagnostic importance.

2.
The Allergic Factor

Allergy means a change in the reaction capacity of the system. It can be introduced either by illness or by the ingestion of a foreign substance. The 'exciting' factor is called the *allergen*. Pollen from hay fields is the allergen in hay fever. The hay fever victim is a typical allergic subject, and the old theory of the pollen from hay being the exciting factor still holds good.

Allergy can develop through being in constant contact with an 'exciting' substance. While normal contact would not produce such allergy, frequent association does tend to bring about the trouble. Drugs, sera, vaccines and certain toilet preparations can induce allergy; even aspirin can produce allergic reactions. In fact, many of the symptoms of allergy are indications that the body is revolting against the presence of foreign substances within the system. In Nature Cure this is interpreted as a natural phenomenon, indicating that the inherent healing powers of the body are actively opposing and expelling the foreign substance. Such indications are normally to be welcomed.

It has been shown that all allergic attacks can be traced to faulty oxidization. A deficiency in the flow of blood permits waste products to accumulate. The accumulation of toxic matter produces spasmodic symptoms in the vascular system, and any deficiency in the supply of oxygen contributes to an allergic attack. It must be remembered, too, that the passing of nerve impulses, upon which all intelligence and co-ordination depend, uses up oxygen. Any lack of oxygen has a direct effect upon the nervous system, this system being the first to react to any impoverishment in the oxygen supply.

The allergic subject displays an acute hypersensitivity. Usually the victim has never known real health, but has always suffered from minor complaints. In real health allergy is unknown. Health, after all, is a state whereby the person is not conscious of any discomfort or even of any organ. It is a state of complete mental and physical harmony.

HEREDITY

Hereditary influences often play a part in disease, particularly where the nervous system is affected. *Allergic parents tend to produce allergic children, and if both parents suffer from allergy the allergic qualities will appear at an early age. Such parents should think very carefully before considering having the child, or children, immunized.* They would be well advised to avoid immunization – a process that Nature Cure rejects as unnecessary, harmful and dangerous.

It is not the intention, however, to lay too much stress on the hereditary factor. Most frequently the same mistakes made by the parents are found in action in their children. Most allergic phenomena are induced by common everyday errors.

The word allergy was coined as recently as 1906, and was recognized in America for a long time before it became a study in this country. While the subject is still more or less in its infancy, it is safe to assume that it is indicative of a lowered vitality and that impoverishment of the blood stream is a concomitant of allergy. Thus improvement in the general health will result in a decrease of the allergy.

3.
The Fallacy of Drug Treatment

One of the tragedies of asthma and hay fever is the failure of orthodox methods to cure the complaints. Medical intervention, we claim, not only fails, but, more than that, retards the recovery and weakens the physical condition.

The victims of asthma and hay fever are only too familiar with the drugs, vaccines, injections, preparations, etc. The majority of these are intended solely for alleviation of the symptoms, and most people do indeed find relief from the agonizing paroxysms by their use.

Although drugs are widely used in the orthodox treatment of asthma, it is well known that drugs are poisonous to the system and may actually cause the asthma. Phenolphthalein, a preparation of phenol, which is used in purgatives, has been known to be one of the causes of asthma. Bromides and aspirin are among the drugs that tend to produce the disease. Sulphonamide, destructive to streptococci and other organisms in the blood, is also among the drugs that may help cause asthma.

Even now, many patent medicines contain drugs that are dangerous to the system, and which are actively concerned in the cause of asthma and hay fever. The person who flies to the chemist for this or that patent medicine is the person who invariably becomes a chronic patient and has to have more frequent recourse to doctors and chemists. Digestive troubles, nerve troubles, colds, etc., (constipation in particular) which are wrongly treated by suppressive or stimulating medicines can lead to bronchial asthma and hay fever.

Drugs that are active agents in the cause of asthma include aspirin and other coal tar products, laxatives, potassium iodide, pyramidon, quinine, bromides, sulphonamides and phenolphthalein. It is a most impressive list illustrating the utter fallacy of drug treatment.

DIGESTION WEAKENED

All drugs and vaccines are produced from drugs or media foreign to the system. The introduction of poisons only adds to the toxic state of the body and further depresses the vitality. Continued orthodox medicinal treatment weakens the digestion — yet the digestion is intimately linked with both asthma and hay fever. The blood stream, already suffering from an accumulation of toxins and carbon dioxide and in an acid condition, is impoverished by an excessive intake of poisons which further reduces the alkalinity of the blood.

Despite the fact that both nerves and tissue require an alkaline medium for healthy functioning — and despite the knowledge that drugs are acid-forming and toxic — such drugs are persisted in for the sake of the transitory relief induced. Such relief, however, is gained only at the expense of a depletion of vital force and makes further attacks more certain. *The disease is not cured — it is the symptoms only that are relieved.*

When, for the sake of temporary relief, poisonous drugs and medicines are administered, the system has to accept an added quota of toxic material. This checks all the vital forces of the body which are striving for health, and adds to the burden of the disease. With resistance lowered because of the increased toxicity of the body, more frequent attacks of greater severity can be expected. This, in turn, leads to the employment of more toxic agents to supply relief, and a vicious circle is created.

INCREASING DOSAGE

Unhappily, however, the system tends to build up a

tolerance towards drugs, so it is soon observed that larger or stronger dosages have to be taken to produce the same amount of relief. In this way the system soon becomes excessively burdened with toxic matter. The result of this is that general health is vastly impaired, the nervous system is depleted, elimination and digestion break down under the strain and the case assumes a chronic and hopeless aspect. The unbroken degeneration in health can lead to an early demise.

The decline in health in asthma and hay fever can often be attributed largely to the habitual use of drugs. The tragic misconception that drugs that give relief will eventually overcome the asthma is proved by the fact that, in the end, the disease is classified as 'incurable.' In the meantime much damage — perhaps permanent damage — has been done to the body.

Drugs and preparations that only suppress and give relief may seem to offer an attractive way out of a temporary difficulty. Superficially they are effective. Since, however, they have only touched upon the symptoms, and the causes still remain, the method is bound to be ineffective. That it is so is proved by the number of asthma sufferers who never respond to drug treatment, but whose health shows a steady degeneration. Drug treatment is a complete fallacy and can never be otherwise.

4 .
Pathology, Symptoms and Causes

Asthma has been defined as 'a recurrent, periodic or paroxysmal type of breathlessness or dyspnoea, character-ised by a wheezing or whistling type of respiration which is associated with marked prolongation of the expiratory phase.' Another definition has been 'an acute oxygen want caused by spasm of the smooth muscles of the finer bronchioles.'

Pathology is the science connected with changes that take place in disease. The pathological findings in asthma are swelling or irregular oedema of the mucous membrane lining the bronchi or bronchioles. The swelling, of course, obstructs the free passage of oxygen to the alveolar spaces. As a result of this, not only is there a want of oxygen, but the carbon dioxide accumulates.

Dyspnoea, or difficult breathing, develops when a person cannot breathe without a certain amount of conscious effort. In the asthmatic this is due to the swelling and obstruction in the air passages in the lungs. It is an expiratory dyspnoea, for, while the forced inspiration takes in oxygen, there is great difficulty in expelling air. The bronchioles, which dilate during forced inspiration, contract during expiration, making it difficult to force out the impure air. This results in a high percentage of carbon dioxide within the lungs and a lack of oxygen. Cynanosis and a sense of suffocation develop from this, and greater efforts are made to relieve the oxygen want.

The cough in asthma is an effort on the part of the lungs to expel the mucopurulent secretion. The origination of the cough is the stimulation of the sensory vagal nerve endings in the lungs or tracheal region. The success of the cough in expelling unwanted substances depends upon the cough reflex and upon the action of the cilia in the bronchioles. The cough, by helping to break up and expel mucus, assists the flow of air to and from the lungs.

The wheezy noises, the cough and other symptoms are due to the presence of mucus within the lungs. The mucus of phlegm which is expectorated is usually clear and frothy, though it is sometimes coloured.

THE VAGUS NERVE

Mention has been made of the vagal nerve endings. These are the nerve endings of the vagus ('wandering') nerve. The vagus nerve is the tenth cranial nerve, and it finds its way into the chest and abdomen. Branches are supplied to the throat, lungs, heart and stomach, etc. It is a very extensive nerve, supplying both sensory and motor functions. That is to say, the vagus nerve not only transmits messages to the brain from the lungs, heart and abdominal organs (the sensory function); it also sends messages to the same organs from the brain, these messages causing a response to changed conditions (the motor function).

The vagus nerve is an important connecting link between the brain and the sympathetic nervous system, which in turn is part of the involuntary nervous system, the system by which muscle, organs and glands that are not under voluntary control are regulated. Blood vessels, stomach and intestines, etc., are supplied with nerves from the sympathetic nervous system.

It will be appreciated, therefore, that the vagus nerve is a very extensive collection of nerve fibres, and it supplies a connection between the heart, lungs and stomach. This makes it easier to understand why an overloaded stomach, for instance, can have a direct influence on asthma and hay fever.

SYMPTOMS

The *symptoms* of asthma are only too familiar to many people. The acute distress is not easily forgotten. As a general rule the onset of an attack is sudden, though premonitory symptoms (depressions, irritability and discomfort) may herald an approach. The asthmatic paroxysm usually asserts itself in the early hours of the morning. The patient awakens in an alarmed and anxious state, with a feeling of tightness and weight, and feels unable to expand his chest.

The actual respiratory embarrassment may be preceded by sneezing or coughing. Acute discomfort is apparent, and respiration is only accomplished with difficulty and produces the wheezing noises characteristic of asthma. The distress increases as the attack proceeds, and the patient tries to sit up with the shoulders raised and head thrown

back, the whole body being torn with the desperate
attempt to breathe. The pulse is rapid and weak, and while
the extremities are cold, the face is wet with perspiration
and either pale or livid. The patient's mind is set on
breathing fresh air, and he will often place himself by an
open window, irrespective of the cold. With the same
desire for freedom and fresh air he loosens his clothing.

The paroxysm lasts for a variable period — maybe for
several hours. The easing of the attack is often marked by
the expectoration of mucus and coughing. As the
breathing becomes easier the patient recovers.

Frequent attacks of asthma are liable to produce
emphysema, which is a condition where there is an
over-distension of the air-cells in the lungs, some destruct-
ion of tissue and the formation of large sacs. These arise
from the rupture or combining together of a number of
adjoining air–vesicles. Bronchial asthma produces
emphysema because, while obstruction prevents air from
being expelled, inspiration is sufficiently forceful to
overcome the obstruction, thus producing distension in the
air cells. With persistent attacks of asthma the distension
causes permanent change in structure and emphysema
results.

Asthma is often associated with bronchitis, nervous
disease and hay fever. Cardiac asthma consists of attacks of
dyspnoea and cyanosis associated with palpitations and
abnormally rapid action of the heart and pulse rate.
Neither cardiac asthma nor renal asthma (difficult
breathing in kidney disease) is a true asthmatic condition.

The symptoms of hay fever are an itching of the eyes
and nose followed by symptoms of a severe cold. There is
violent sneezing and a profuse watery discharge from the
eyes and nose. A dry cough and asthmatical paroxysms
arise. The condition springs from an inflamed state of the
mucous membranes of the eyes, nose and air passages. It is
associated with asthma, but is usually only effective from
May to July inclusive. Rhinitis (a catarrhal condition of
the nose, often influenced by malformation of the bony

structure of the nose) makes certain subjects liable to an attack of hay fever. The chronic inflammation of the mucous membranes of the nose in rhinitis is similar to part of the symptoms in hay fever and is conducive to hay fever.

THE CAUSES

What are the causes of asthma and hay fever? Fundamentally the causes can be summed up in two words: *wrong living*.

Undoubtedly allergy plays a big part, particularly with hay fever. It is often proved, however, that when all the supposedly offending substances are removed from the diet or environment the disease is still unchecked. Removal from the countryside, for instance, during the fatal months in hay fever often brings no relief. It is quite true, of course, that pollens and fumes can travel varying distances, making it a difficult task to escape some offending causes. The avoidance of certain allergen foods (usually eggs, shell-fish, strawberries, pork, tomatoes, etc.,) does not always alleviate the condition. It is extremely difficult to escape from dust and animal emanations, and one can change all the pillows and cushions in the house with no visible effect upon either asthma or hay fever.

In some cases striking results can be achieved when, perhaps, the allergic factor is the dominant aspect, and the allergen is removed. In the vast majority of cases, however, the allergic subject, as previously mentioned, is already susceptible to ill-health and possesses a lowered resistance. He is, therefore, an easy victim to disease and, because of the peculiar nature of allergy, has a typical asthma and hay fever proclivity. The nervous derangement, allied to the physical weakness, makes the allergic person susceptible to asthma and hay fever.

The spasmodic contraction of the smaller bronchial tubes is the chief item in asthma. The derangement of the nervous system, acting, directly or by reflex action, on the nerves supplying the muscular fibres of the bronchi and regulating their calibre, is responsible for the terrifying paroxysms. The nervous element in allergy — which is often present in asthma and always a feature of hay fever lies not only in the stimulation of the sensory nerve endings, but also in the psychic field.

The neurotic elements in asthma and hay fever are a constant reminder of the pressure of modern living. It has been proved that nervous stimuli do occasion asthmatical attacks. Worry, fright, anger and excessive exuberation will produce true asthmatical paroxysms in the diseased person. Psychoneurosis is not essential to asthma, but it is often present.

By itself the neurotic element is probably insufficient to *cause* asthma or hay fever. It is, however, a strong enough factor either to initiate an attack in the person already suffering from the disease, or to aggravate the diseased condition. One is unable to escape from the conclusion that nervous troubles predispose to asthma and hay fever and that the nervous element can arise at an early age or be influenced by hereditary traits. Psychoneurosis must be considered an etiological factor in asthma and hay fever. The fact must not be overlooked, however, that depression from constant asthmatical attacks tends to produce neurotic tendencies.

PSYCHOSOMATICS

Asthma and hay fever can be classified as psychosomatic disorders. Tension, invariably present in such conditions, is eased when the ability to relax is increased. One of the finest ways of relaxing is to lie flat on the floor, without even a pillow for the head. In this position stretch out the limbs and then endeavour to relax all the muscles of the body. Combine this with deep-breathing after relaxing. Inhale as deeply as possible, using only the diaphragm, raising the wall of the abdomen without raising the lower abdomen or chest. Allow about four seconds for inhalation and almost twice as long for exhalation.

Relaxing and deep-breathing should be carried out quite

frequently, and especially when any sensation of tension or fatigue is experienced and an opportunity to relax presents itself.

The embarrassed respiration from the changes in calibre of the bronchi, the expectoration of phlegm and the irritation of the mucous membranes lining the air passages indicate a catarrhal condition of the body. Catarrh is often the forerunner of both asthma and hay fever – especially when the catarrhal condition is linked with the nervous and allergic elements. The catarrh may be present, and often is, not only in the chest but in the stomach and all the alimentary tract. Because of the intimate connections via the vagus nerve, gastric distress caused by an accumulation of mucus in the stomach can initiate an attack of asthma. When catarrh of the stomach is present it is likely that it will also be felt in the lungs and air passages. Any accumulation of mucus, therefore, predisposes to asthma and hay fever.

SHALLOW BREATHING

We have mentioned that faulty oxidization is a feature of allergy. This arises from various sources. One obvious factor is shallow breathing. By making insufficient use of the lungs the body is at once deprived of vital oxygen and the carbon dioxide content of the blood is allowed to rise.

Shallow breathing can be just as much a habit as eating or drinking. It is often the outcome of a sedentary life, but the habit of not using the lungs to even an approximation of their full capacity is decidedly harmful. It is, in effect, the equivalent of always living in a stuffy, airless atmosphere. It makes for fatigue, headaches, lassitude, depression and insomnia. Shallow breathing curtails the revitalizing of the blood-stream and helps to create an acid system. The decreased vitality resulting from inadequate oxidization lessens resistance to disease. Any bronchial attack in such a condition, treated in the orthodox allopathic manner, can lead to bronchial asthma.

A second cause of faulty oxidization is insufficient

elimination via the skin. Apart from the secretions of the sweat glands, by which toxins are eliminated, the skin also gives off a certain amount of gases. If the skin is not permitted to function because it has been depleted by neglect, over-protection by thick and tight clothing or by too intensive heat (over-hot fires or very hot baths) the toxins normally eliminated via the skin remain in the system. Retention of poisons because of reduced skin activity causes faulty oxidization and acidity.

Constipation is another contributory factor to asthma and hay fever. If not a permanent state, constipation must have existed for a considerable period. Many unsuspecting people suffering from constipation cause their own asthma and hay fever by *attempting* to cure their costiveness with the use of patent laxatives and purges. They do not, of course, cure the constipation, or the constant taking of such purges would be unnecessary.

What they do achieve is the forcing of a bowel movement at the expense of natural functioning. This produces weakness of the bowels and addiction to stronger and stronger doses of laxatives. Ultimately they become addicts to chronic constipation (with all it means in the retention of poisons and acid system) and take sufficient of one drug or another to produce asthma in an already weakened body. The basic cause of constipation, as a general rule, lies in a lifelong failure to obey the laws of nature, both as regards diet and living and in the mechanical over-stimulation — leading to malfunction — of a natural process.

OVER-EATING

Over-eating and over-drinking are concerned in the causation of asthma and hay fever. Any excesses in diet, creating an overloaded stomach, can initiate an attack of asthma. Previous to the actual onset of the disease, however, the detrimental effect of indulgences is insidious. The temporary discomfort originally felt after injudicious eating and drinking was merely a warning that the system rebelled against such treatment. However temporary the discomfort appeared, there was a certain amount of damage wrought and poisons accumulated. The constant disregarding of such warnings permits a cumulative rise in toxins, a more extensive damage to the nervous system and, ultimately, the appearance of asthma and hay fever.

POSTURE

Posture receives scant attention in the etiology of asthma and hay fever, yet it does merit some thought. It is realized that the main feature in the diseases is the disturbance in the respiratory mechanism. The importance of making full use of the lungs can hardly be over-emphasized, yet few people use their lungs to the best advantage. It is equally apparent that many occupations involve positions that do not admit proper freedom for the ribs to move, thus making expansion of the lungs difficult.

Sitting or standing erect, or even lying flat, does permit that mobility of the chest essential to full oxygenation of the blood stream. The slouching or slumping-over attitude compresses the lungs, the diaphragm and abdomen, and inhibits or curtails visceral movements which normally take place during full respiration. When posture interferes with correct breathing, as is so often the case, there is an accumulation of carbon dioxide which looms so largely in the weakened condition, and in the etiology of diseases of the nervous system.

Bad posture serves to cause or increase neuro-muscular tension, owing to the strain on certain sets of muscles, and the weakness from misuse of all the musculature concerned in the respiratory function. This tension is nearly always found in the head, neck, shoulders, ribs and spine. Contraction and lack of mobility are particularly evident in the cervical and thoracic regions of the spine and in the ribs and intercostal muscles. Such tension, arising from bad posture, plays a vital part in the cause of asthma and hay fever.

To a large extent posture is influenced by health, as well

as having an influence on health. It will be appreciated by now that the typical allergic subject is a person with subnormal health. Such a person is more easily fatigued and, therefore, more likely to slump. When he does permit the slackness in posture he is surely accelerating the onset of asthma and hay fever. There exists, therefore, a train of events leading to the actual onset of the diseases, bad posture being an item in the list of causes.

There are, of course, certain aspects in the causation of asthma and hay fever which in these days it would be difficult to eradicate. Often a change of occupation is necessary. Industrial fumes, coal gases, obnoxious vapour, etc., all have an irritating effect upon the lungs. Chemical irritations from fumes in steel works, for instance, may involve a change in occupation before any improvement could be hoped for.

It would be extremely difficult to escape from all the irritating factors that tend to produce asthma and hay fever. It is, however, possible to recognize the inherent dangers and to build a bulwark against them. Such a bulwark is the development of general health to such a pitch that asthma and hay fever need never be contracted.

AEROSOL SPRAYS

An increasing hazard to health – which is of particular interest to asthmatics and allergic subjects – is the wide-spread use of aerosols of all types. These are not confined to insect sprays, but include polishes, hair sprays, etc.

Asthma and hay fever have a relation to skin diseases. Some cosmetics are suspect, and any person who displays an allergic reaction to hair sprays or cosmetics should promptly abandon the offending media. In any event, great care should be taken if and when a hair spray (or any type of chemical or cosmetic spray) is used.

Petrol and diesel fumes are a definite source of air pollution, but the use of a great many of the present-day aerosols, which, in any case, are usually applied in confined spaces and in close proximity, can be equally dangerous.

Asthma and hay fever are not the outcome of any one possible cause. They are the result of the multiplication of sufficient adverse factors in the daily routine. These so influence health that it is difficult to escape the diseases. Any one or more factors may have a larger responsibility than others, *but no one item alone is sufficient in itself to produce the asthma or hay fever*. Thus it would be quite easy to discard – or escape from – all the allergens deemed responsible, and still suffer. *This is often the case and is responsible, along with drug treatment, for the so-called 'incurability' of asthma and hay fever.*

The causes of asthma and hay fever can be listed as: allergy, bad diet, excesses, worry, fear, nervous debility, drugs, constipation, environment, occupational irritants, bad posture, heriditary influences, lack of exercise, shallow breathing, tobacco, etc. Not all may be present in any one case, but a combination of some of the above must be considered in every person who suffers from asthma and hay fever.

5.
Diet as a Cause

A close study of the diet question reveals an amazing phenomena, and this is not so much the amount of illness that prevails in all civilized countries, but the way the human organism strives to overcome all the handicaps and abuses to which it is subject. It speaks a great deal for the tenacity and power of the inherent healing forces of the body that they can survive the treatment meted out day by day, year in and year out.

Many of the abuses regarding food are difficult to avoid, for they begin, not at the dining table, but in the soil.

Every person must be aware that the average food-producing farm, market garden or orchard uses vast amounts of chemical fertilisers and sprays. The fertilisers are intended primarily for the purpose of producing more food per acre, but this object is achieved at the expense of the soil, *and in the actual food value of the produce.*

The whole world exists on a few inches of soil. Those few inches of top soil spell the difference between wholesale starvation and a world of plenty. Top soil's most vital constituent is known as *humus.* Humus is the product of the decomposition of animal and vegetable residues by the active work of micro-organisms. It is, therefore, a living force that provides the soil with all its goodness. This process is assisted by worms which aerate and otherwise improve the soil. The soil, therefore, is organic and full of life. Chemical fertilisers are inorganic 'boosters.' These chemicals stimulate the soil to such a degree that crops are abundant. They do not, however, add anything to the land, and they do tend to kill the worms and other live matter. Also, and this is important, over-stimulation produces weakness.

Ultimately the chemical fertilisers kill the life of the soil and destroy the micro-organisms. The humus is dissipated, since, by the law of return, nothing but chemicals are added to the soil, when its real requirements are animal and vegetable residues to restore the humus. Intensive cultivation by modern artificial methods may produce larger crops for a period, but these crops are of inferior food value, and the inevitable result of such treatment is a *spent* soil. In this way the *dust-bowls* of the future are created.

We have to contend therefore with a deficiency in food value before we take account of all the other factors involved in the maltreatment of food.

WHITE FLOUR AND SUGAR
Not satisfied with the intensive cultivation of inferior food, we have to again suffer from further tampering at

the hands of commercialism. Quite a lot has already been said, from time to time, about the way wheat is misused. The commercial milling of flour has led to all sorts of minor complaints and deficiencies.

With the growth of population and industry, the concentration of flour interests into fewer and fewer hands, and the need for centralization and increased production it has been necessary to find some means of overcoming the obstacles associated with stone-milling. The largest objections to the old method were its limitations in dealing with quantities and the old argument that stone-ground flour did not keep.

The introduction of the steel-roller mill was a boon to the milling interests, but a death-blow to national health. For efficient functioning, modern milling methods discard the wheat germ and the bran. The wheat germ contains the vitamins and mineral salts essential to the maintenance of health. Vitamin E is lost when the wheat germ is discarded; as well as vital sources of Vitamin B. Wholewheat contains all the elements from which the body is made, yet it is indiscriminately tampered with. Bran, the roughage of wheat, is also discarded during the milling process, later to be sold as medicinal food or given to livestock. The removal of the bran is one of the measures largely responsible for the creation of constipation on the mass scale that now prevails.

White flour, therefore, is little more than a filling, glutinous mass, from which most of the natural elements have been taken. With them go the resistance to disease, and no amount of artificial vitamin addition ever replaces the natural elements.

White sugar, also, is really a travesty of a food. From the original pure cane practically all the vitamins and mineral salts are removed during the refining process. All that is left is a highly concentrated and acid-forming food that is detrimental to health. Most certainly white sugar contains calories but, as a highly concentrated food, it produces catarrh, acidity and dental decay.

Since a great many foods contain both white flour and white sugar, plus artificial flavourings and chemical adulterations, it is possible to obtain a small insight into the enormous amount of damage food suffers at the hands of commercialism. It must be reiterated that these depradations play a large part in the cause of asthma and hay fever.

MILK

Milk is a valuable source of Vitamins A, D and C. Although it is to be debated whether or not milk is a good adult food (it is very mucus-forming) these vitamins are useful to health. All vitamins, particularly Vitamin C, are susceptible to heat treatment. During pasteurization much of the Vitamin C is destroyed. Milk is also a valuable source of calcium (necessary for bone formation), yet a lot of this is left behind during the act of pasteurizing.

What are the arguments for pasteurization? Mainly that it enables clean, safe milk to be left at the door. The clean, safe milk is full of dead germs and, in large towns, that same milk was probably collected three days previous to delivery. Pasteurization is nothing more or less than a convenience. It covers up the delivery of stale milk, inefficient collection methods and diseased herds. Pasteurization and refrigeration are merely useful means of overcoming some of the difficulties inherited with the industrial era.

Up to now, only the ill-effects that food suffers *before* it reaches the household have been considered. What further damaging processes food undergoes depends upon the knowledge, prejudice or willingness of the housewife. And remember that all this time an inspection of the factors vitally concerned is being made, not only in the causation of asthma and hay fever, but in the cause of a thousand and one ailments from which humanity suffers. Diet is a tremendous force either for health or against it; for if the food we consume is poisoned and deficient, so must our bodies be poisoned and deficient. If the food is predominantly acid, then the blood-stream will be predominantly acid. Yet, for health, the system requires an alkaline blood-stream.

THE COMPOSITION OF FOOD

Food is necessary for the growth and repair of tissue and for the provision of energy. It should be enjoyed, but its primary function is to maintain all life forces. The food we consume is composed of proteins, starches, sugars, fats, vitamins, mineral salts, roughage and water. All are essential, in proper proportions, to the harmonious working of the body. Unfortunately the common mistake, to which most people subscribe, is the undue emphasis on proteins, fats and starches. For normal purposes, therefore, food is again broken down into two combinations — one acid, the other alkaline.

Proteins contain nitrogen, which is essential for the growth and repair of all the cells of the body. While proteins are obtainable from animal and vegetable matter, the first-named is the most prolific source. Meat, fish, eggs, cheese, milk and nuts give most proteins. Nitrogen is not stored in the body, and the waste products from the protein are taken to the liver by the blood, where urea is formed. Any excess of protein causes an accumulation of uric acid.

Carbohydrates contain carbon and combine with oxygen to provide heat and energy. Carbohydrates are composed of sugars and starches, and the most common sources are wheat, barley, rice, maize, potatoes, sugar, bananas, etc. Bread, sugar and potatoes are the most familiar carbohydrate foods. Cakes, cornflour, pastries etc., are practically all carbohydrate. Carbohydrates are broken down during digestion and stored in the liver and muscles.

Fats come from animal or vegetable products. Meat, dairy produce, olive oil, seed oils, fish oil, nuts, etc., are familiar examples of fat. Fat is stored in the body as adipose tissue and forms a reserve store of energy.

Mineral Salts are the chemical elements from which the

body is made. All the cells of the body require mineral salts. The best known are *calcium*, for bone; *iron*, for the blood; *sodium chloride*, for the gastric juices; *iodine*, for the thyroid gland; and *sulphur*, for the bile and liver. Including oxygen, the body is, to all practical purposes, made up of sixteen chemical elements. The mineral salts found in food form the chief items, apart from the oxygen. Meat and fish contain mineral salts, but the best sources are vegetables, fruit, nuts and edible seaweed.

Vitamins are mysterious elements found in minute quantities in most foods. Vitamin deficiency results in rickets, lowered resistance, nervous troubles, skin diseases, sterility, bleeding, etc. Vitamins enable fats and oils to be utilized by the body. The best sources are dairy produce, fruit, vegetables and sunshine. Synthetic vitamins should be disregarded, as it is highly improbable that artificial methods can reproduce the exact article.

Both vitamins and mineral salts form only a minute part of food. Without either the body is unable to exist. It is only within the last seventy years or so that vitamins or mineral salts have been regarded as of any importance, but it is only within the last seventy years or so that it has been necessary to think of them at all. Previously food was not contaminated or tampered with either in growth or in preparation, and for the ordinary person there was no need to consider either. Now that it is vitally necessary to consider both vitamins and mineral salts, they are found to be too often neglected, especially the mineral salts.

Water forms about two-thirds of the weight of the body and is contained in food to approximately the same extent. Bread contains water 36 per cent, meat 70 per cent, cheese 34 per cent, fish 80 per cent, and fruits and vegetables from 75 to over 90 per cent. Even an ordinary, unbalanced diet, therefore, will contain about 75 per cent water. Only habit and the prolific use of thirst-promoting condiments make much tea and coffee drinking desirable to the ordinary person, thought it must be stated here and now that both tea and coffee have *no* food value and are harmful beverages.

ACID/ALKALI BALANCE

It is necessary to go to some length on the question of diet because it raises such problems and brings important influences to bear on the causes and cure of asthma and hay fever. This raises the question of the acid and alkaline elements in diet. Remember that for health to be maintained at a proper level it is absolutely imperative that the alkalinity of the blood-stream be assured. An unbalanced diet can set up a vicious circle which is highly detrimental to health.

The relative alkalinity of the fluid medium of the body decides the state of the health. There are, of course, other factors in the cause of asthma and hay fever, which have previously been referred to. In the main, however, since wrong diet and a preponderance of acid-forming materials sets up a whole chain of detrimental factors, it is the question of diet that absorbs so much of our interest.

Broadly speaking, the alkaline foods are the fruits and vegetables; the acid-forming foods, proteins, carbohydrates (starches and sugars) and fats. This division is the vital point where most dietetic mistakes are made. We have come to regard proteins and carbohydrates as the two important essentials in food. Both are, of course, essential to physical well-being, but not in the proportions to which civilization has become accustomed. And, moreover, one must always consider those denaturing processes that accompany the carbohydrate group in particular (refining, milling, chemical adulteration, etc.).

Bread is a carbohydrate — as such it is used to a vast extent because it is a cheap *filling* food. The ordinary loaf, however, is seriously deficient in natural elements, apart from having chemical additions to improve its *whiteness*. The bran taken from the wheat causes wholesale constipation, the lack of vitamins causes nervous diseases and sterility, etc. Both constipation and nervous debility are serious contributory factors in asthma and hay fever. This is particularly so when, to relieve the constipation, medicinal purges are employed. Constipation in itself is a serious failure in the human economy, because it means nothing more nor less than a retention of toxins. These toxins accumulate in the bloodstream and tissues, causing lethargy, headaches, poor circulation and lowered vitality.

Bread — or excess of other starch foods — is both acid and mucus-forming. Catarrh is a common complaint of the person who eats masses of white bread or white flour products (or even too many wholewheat products). Catarrh is a symptom common to asthma and hay fever. It arises in the mucous membranes lining the air-passages and causes severe irritation and inflammation.

Note how only one aspect in diet can create several conditions favourable to the establishment of asthma and hay fever; also that orthodox drug measures to overcome the complaints arising from a bad diet tend to produce more serious disease.

White sugar is a highly refined, denatured food product. It is a very concentrated food which, when taken in any quantity, produces symptoms of catarrh. It is acid-forming and creates mucus. Cakes and pastries, chocolates and any food that is largely composed of white flour or white sugar or a combination of both are inimical to the healthy state.

Carbohydrates are necessary, the quantity varying with age, amount of energy used in work and exercise, general physique, etc. The best sources are wholewheat bread and wholegrain cereals, potatoes, honey and dates.

MEAT

It has long been established that the amount of protein necessary to health could be considerably reduced from what is generally regarded as essential. The erroneous myth that flesh food is a dire necessity dies hard. All proteins are acid-forming. Meat is a very bad example of protein. Apart from any normal consideration of acidity, it is capable of causing intestinal putrefaction. In the ordinary person existing on an unbalanced diet, there is frequently a constipated state. Any undue delay in the evacuation of the end-products of meat consumption creates a putrefaction which is a factor in the cause of asthma and hay fever. Pork, for instance, should never be consumed by the asthmatic.

Meat products are acid-forming, though not all to the same degree. Chicken is less harmful than bacon or beef, but fresh fish is best, though it is often not tolerated by the asthma and hay fever victim. Sausages, a mixture of meat, bread and spices, etc., are particularly bad, and more so because they generally have to be fried.

The best sources of protein foods are eggs, milk, cheese, butter, nuts and, occasionally, light meat or fish. Not one of these items should ever be fried. It must be noted, too, that cheese and milk are mucus-forming and may add to the catarrhal condition. Sour milk or junket is preferred to ordinary milk, and cheese should be consumed in moderate quantities. Cooked cheese dishes should only be taken with care. In any event, all protein foods should be taken sparingly. It is surprising how little protein foods are really required, and great physiological economy can be assured by reducing the protein intake.

The common excesses of carbohydrates and proteins are largely responsible for the many ailments of civilization. They form the largest single factor in the cause of catarrh, constipation, gastric distress, nervous disorders, etc. From these complaints springs a tendency to asthma and hay fever.

TEA, COFFEE AND ALCOHOL

The acid-forming food materials do not end in meat, white flour and white sugar. Tea, coffee and alcohol are also responsible for the formation of acid products. All these beverages are stimulants which have an unfavourable reaction upon the system. Take the early morning cup of tea, for example. On rising, there is very often a heavy feeling resulting from poisons circulating in the bloodstream. These poisons have been drawn from the tissues during sleep. This toxic matter should be eliminated as early as possible, preferably with the aid of exercise, water, orange or other fruit juice to stimulate the bowels and kidneys. Instead of that a cup of tea is imbibed. Under the stimulus of the tea, the poisons are immediately thrust back into the tissues and the heavy feeling is relieved. A bowel action may or may not result from drinking the tea, but the floating poisons are still driven into the tissues to await a further call for elimination.

Numerous cups of tea or coffee seriously interfere with digestion and add to the acidity of the body. Such drinks have no food value, they are merely stimulants. Drinking with meals, in particular, is extremely harmful to the digestion. It causes an overloaded stomach (often concerned in asthma and hay fever), dilutes the gastric juices, throws unnecessary work upon the kidneys and bladder and generally causes havoc with the nervous system and heart. Only the astonishing resilience of the human organism saves the body from extensive damage. However, such excursions into influences harmful to the body do have their ultimate effect in reducing the vital forces of the organism.

APPETIZERS

Pickles, sauces, condiments, etc., are the outcome of a depraved taste. They are meant to stimulate and provoke thirst and appetite. By their habitual use it is quite easy to eat and drink far beyond the real requirements. Over-eating, particularly of foods already detrimental to the system, piles up the amount of toxins ingested with every meal. It taxes the digestion and places a severe strain on the already over-burdened organs of elimination. All pickles, condiments, etc., are acid-forming and injurious to the body, apart from leading to excesses in food and drink.

If food were grown and prepared in relation to natural laws, these added incentives to eat and drink would not be required. The natural taste in the ordinary person is weakened by years of addiction to synthetic food preparations and bad cooking methods. When appetite flags, such articles as pickles, sauces, condiments and other impediments of the culinary art are adopted to revive and stimulate the interest in food and drink. Such means become common habit and lead to excesses.

COMMON MISTAKES

A normal, orthodox meal is riddled with mistakes and excesses and is entirely unbalanced and deficient in real food value. A breakfast of bacon or sausages, fried bread or porridge and toast, butter and marmalade, washed down with cups of tea or coffee to which white sugar has been added, has little real food value. It is, of course, crammed with calories to provide energy. The protein content is probably too large (it would be much larger still if bacon and eggs were taken in any quantity), and a certain amount of roughage is present.

On the whole, however, it contains little or no vitamin and mineral element and is excessively acid-forming. What is more, since little work has been performed either during sleep or after awakening, there is no real need for such a breakfast. It is not the result of hunger so much as the result of habit.

Lunch is probably of meat or fish and boiled-out potatoes and soggy cabbage or other greens with either a bread-and-butter or rice pudding or fruit and custard or pastry. It is usually followed by tea or coffee. Here, again, the emphasis is on carbohydrates and proteins, and is once more a mainly acid-forming meal. Almost invariably, what alkaline fruits or vegetables are consumed have lost their vitamins and mineral salts (or a large proportion of them) in the cooking process.

Tea, of course, includes tea, bread and butter and cakes or pastries. It is an entirely acid and mucus-forming repast calculated to produce catarrh and toxaemia. It is, too, an unnecessary meal.

Supper is usually a mixture of tea and lunch — probably a lighter meal, but still containing an excess of carbohydrates and proteins. If we examine a normal light supper of bread and butter, meat or fish or egg, tea or coffee, it is again acid and mucus-forming. If more than a moderate meal is consumed, especially at a late hour, then the eater retires with an overloaded stomach. In such a state, together with a system over-burdened with toxins, conditions are favourable for an attack of asthma.

It will, by now, be appreciated that orthodox eating habits show a lamentable disregard for the fundamentals of diet. There is a complete lack of balance; an excess of acid and mucus-forming foods, a serious deficiency in alkaline foods, loss of vitamins and mineral salts by ignorance in cooking and the addition of stimulating drinks and condiments. Further damage is often caused by lack of mastication and eating when under emotional or nervous strain and when tired.

The picture that has been painted is somewhat more than gloomy. It is, however, based on solid facts. Only the extraordinary resilience of the human organism, and its great capacity to adapt itself to environment thus compensating for abuses, saves it from more disease than it encounters. As it is, the great majority of people depend upon a series of colds, catarrh, acne and other eliminatory flare-ups to expel accumulated poisons. When these are suppressed by drugs, chronic conditions arise. Is it surprising, therefore, that a state of half health — half disease is the most prevailing condition? *The diet factor, more than anything else, is responsible for the incidence of asthma and hay fever.*

6.
Diet as a Cure

From what has been said in the last section, it will be quite obvious that the cure for asthma and hay fever lies largely in the reduction of acid and mucus-forming foods and in the increase of the alkaline element in diet. It will be equally plain that the acid foods are the proteins, starches, sugars and fats, the alkaline foods being mainly fruit and vegetables – and these partly in the raw state. That, in the main, is the simple division.

From what we have learnt about the chemical adulteration, refining and other causes of vitamin and mineral loss, however, we must take more care to ensure that further denaturing of food is kept to a minimum. In this connection we must stress the importance of raw food and steaming, baking, casserole and conservative cooking. Raw food avoids practically all loss of vitamins and mineral salts.

The methods of cooking mentioned reduce the damage to food to a minimum. Since it is of vital importance to reduce losses of vitamins and mineral salts to fractional proportions, raw feeding takes on a special significance. Dr Bircher-Benner, the late eminent dietitian, insisted that, for correct feeding, 50 per cent of all food consumed should be eaten in the raw state.

Thus a further division is made. The emphasis is now upon the alkaline fruits and vegetables, with as much as 50 per cent of this in raw food form. Why so much emphasis on raw food? In the first place – and this is quite distinct from any consideration of vitamin and mineral loss – raw feeding helps to obviate any danger of over-eating. Over-eating is often concerned in asthma and hay fever. This could be the case, though with less deleterious effects, even on a balanced diet. Raw food, however, reduces this danger.

Raw food requires more mastication than is normally devoted to cooked food. The extensive chewing needed to reduce raw food to a swallowable state satisfies the hunger more effectively. Thus, as a simple illustration, three raw carrots would give the same satisfaction as six cooked carrots of the same size.

A BALANCED DIET

A typical balanced diet should roughly consist of whole-grain cereals in low quantities (*i.e.* wholewheat bread, brown rice, barley, etc.), fruit and vegetables in abundance with half of them in the raw state, dairy produce in fair quantities and nuts and natural sugars and oils in low quantities. Much depends upon the amount of energy normally used, but the proteins and carbohydrates should always be kept at low proportions. Even quite hard physical work can be performed on a diet that includes only limited amounts of proteins and carbohydrates.

The victim of asthma and hay fever must, at all costs, drastically reduce the intake of acid and mucus-forming food materials. Even the normal diet, apart from any consideration of the more drastic curative efforts, should always emphasize the alkaline fruits and vegetables, with particular reference to the raw foods. The following is a sample weekly menu:

1	2	3
Breakfast	*Breakfast*	*Breakfast*
Muesli	Stewed prunes	Orange
	Wheatgerm	Berry fruit
	Raw apple	
Lunch	*Lunch*	*Lunch*
Poached egg on spinach	Baked potato and butter	Mushrooms
Grilled tomatoes	Cauliflower	Swede *or* turnip
One potato (large)	Leeks *or* onion	Carrots

Baked apple or Fruit jelly	Junket	Dried fruit

4	5	6
Breakfast	*Breakfast*	*Breakfast*
Muesli	Prunes or figs	Grapefruit
	Little cereal	Apple
		Few dates
Lunch	*Lunch*	*Lunch*
Cauliflower au gratin	Baked potato and	Grilled tomatoes
Onions	butter	Fresh peas or
Steamed potatoes	Spinach	beans
	Carrots	Steamed potatoes
Baked apple	Dried fruit	Fruit jelly

7
Breakfast: Muesli.
Lunch: Nut loaf.
        Greens. Carrots.
        Prunes.

The *tea* meal in all cases should be of fruit juice only, but weak tea could be permitted now and again. Nothing to eat.

Supper (same throughout): 1 slice wholemeal bread and butter or toast and butter or biscuits and butter. Raw salad. Tablespoonful grated cheese. Fresh fruit (*i.e.* apple, berry fruit, peaches, grapes, orange or grapefruit, etc.).

The preparation of the *muesli* begins overnight by soaking one tablespoonful of porridge oats in two to three tablespoonfuls of water. In the morning add one large raw grated apple (or same quantity of chopped prunes or mixed fruit), two tablespoonfuls of milk and a few drops of lemon or orange juice. Add honey or molasses to taste. The muesli is not cooked and makes a delicious breakfast dish.

It must be noted, incidentally, that some asthmatics may not be able to take nuts either milled or made into such savouries as nut roasts, etc.

The *raw salad* should not contain more than five of the fresh salad foods in season. The usual items are: carrots, cauliflower, celery, cress, cabbage, beetroot, endive, lettuce, spinach, leeks, onions, swede, tomatoes, turnip, watercress, nasturtiums, dandelion, parsley, thyme, chives, mint, etc., can all be added as natural seasonings. .

Salad dressing should consist of olive oil and lemon juice only. Salt and vinegar must never be used. The addition of any grated cheese or nuts to the salad must depend upon two factors: firstly, the individual ability to take cheese without causing too much mucus and, secondly, whether the grated or milled nuts cause irritation in the ailmentary tract. Chestnut puree is acceptable, however, and a small glass of sour milk or yogurt could be added to the salad meal.

The last meal should never be later than seven in the evening. Any drink taken after that time should be a small drink — preferably apple or orange juice with carrageen moss added.

No change in the order of the meals is advised. It would be an advantage to make the evening meal as light as possible. Any beverages (fruit juices, dandelion coffee, maté tea, yeast extract, etc.,) should be taken independently of meals. If thirst is not present, it is not necessary to drink, and late drinking should be avoided. The carrageen moss which is added to fruit drinks should also be used when preparing fruit jellies. It is invaluable in the treatment of asthma and other respiratory ailments.

Some people find that an early morning drink is helpful to the bowels. In these cases, the best drinks are warm prune, raisin or orange juice. With the diet possessing such a large water content, however, the amount of fluid required is considerably reduced. Any fluid taken in excess of real requirements means extra work for the body.

It is to be emphasized that the diet outlines is one for general purposes. The more drastic measures for eliminating toxins and curing the asthma and hay fever will be outlined subsequently. The diet regime will certainly cure constipation and many minor ailments. It will raise the standard of general health and strengthen the resistance to disease. It is, however, only for normal living purposes, following upon the more severe measures to be undertaken to cleanse the system. Undoubtedly such a diet regime will remove all the results of former indiscretions and build up a high level of personal health. It can, too, be made more generous as the cure of asthma and hay fever becomes more certain.

Personal idiosyncracies must be taken into account until the disease is cured. If any unnatural reactions arise as a result of consuming eggs, fish or cheese, etc., then these must be banned from the diet. Any deficiencies can be made up from the other items. While all fruits should be taken as a normal rule, rhubarb is an exception and must never be consumed.

7.
The Benefits of Fasting

The first essential in the cure of asthma and hay fever is to remove the toxins from the system. One of the basic laws of Nature Cure is *remove the cause*, and fasting is one of the best means of obeying this law. No method is so speedy, so efficient or so correct as fasting. Given time, fasting will eliminate all the poisonous end-products of years of wrong living. Therapeutic fasting prevents any ingestion of toxic products and releases all the life forces of the body for the task of eliminating effete matter. The whole digestive system enjoys a rest, and the energy normally devoted to the act of digestion and assimilation is diverted to the purpose of eliminating poisons.

No one would argue that fasting is pleasant, but it is not so difficult, dangerous or unpleasant as is commonly assumed. The worst difficulty is to overcome the habit of eating. The second difficulty is boredom.

The idea that without food the body will be weakened is true only in part. Therapeutic fasting is as sane as eating.

It is, in fact, a natural instinct that is suppressed by fear. Loss of appetite is, ninety-nine times out of a hundred, a safety precaution. The body rebels against food and desires and seeks an opportunity to cleanse itself. The digestive system requires a rest, and the healing powers of the body wish to express themselves. This phenonmenon is typically witnessed in colds and fevers. Here we have classical examples of anorexia (loss of appetite) combined with supra-normal activity. The system does not require food because it is already fully occupied in throwing our or burning up poisons. To force food down at such a time is stupid in that it is not only repugnant to the person, but it also inhibits the cleansing process.

A NATURAL PROCESS

Controlled, therapeutic fasting, therefore, is a natural process. Many people fast for as long a period as thirty to forty days, and without distress. Any fasting over five days, however, should be carried out under expert supervision. Up to five days it should be quite safe to fast at home. Over that point it is advisable either to have expert supervision or to enter a Nature Cure establishment, where fasting and treatment will do much towards cleansing the system and curing asthma and hay fever. Indeed, fasting is the only speedy medium of disencumbering the system of the results of years of wrong living and drug treatment in a manner consistent with natural laws.

The fast may be conducted on water, or it may be carried out with a combination of such drinks as: orange juice, apple juice, raisin juice, prune juice, maté tea, lemon juice, grapefruit juice, yeast extract or clear vegetable broth. Drinks may be taken every two to three hours. The fruit juice should be diluted with water. No solid food whatsoever is taken.

The best plan is to commence the fast with a teaspoonful of Epsom salts dissolved in a little lukewarm water, taken together with a large glass of lukewarm water. Repeat this dose half an hour later. One dose of Epsom salts is taken on the second day of the fast, and may be repeated on subsequent days on a short fast. In the place of Epsom salts or some other aperient water may be taken.

The idea of the aperient (not normally advised in Nature Cure) is to stimulate the bowels at the beginning of the fast. This, in itself, is insufficient, and it is necessary to have recourse to the enema — either daily or every other day — so long as the fast persists. The bowel cleansing is essential because of the drastic cleansing process that is in progress throughout the system. Toxins are being drawn from all over the body and it is imperative that these toxins be eliminated as quickly as possible to ensure the efficacy of the fast. Any undue delay in the removal of the toxic products would not only hinder the purpose of the fast, but it may mean that some toxins would be re-absorbed into the blood-stream. Bowel cleansing helps to mitigate or overcome some of the disagreeable symptoms associated with fasting.

SYMPTOMS OF FASTING

A thickly coated tongue, bad breath, headache and, possibly, some disturbance of sleep, may arise from fasting. The coated tongue and bad breath are almost inevitable. All the symptoms, however, can be relieved, to some extent, by the use of the enema.

Not all symptoms are unpleasant. There are many good signs associated with fasting. There is, quite frequently, a feeling of lightness and well-being which has never been experienced previously. Quite a large number of people can do hard work and take long walks even after days of fasting. In asthma and hay fever it often produces a sense of physical comfort unknown in normal existence.

Hot and cold hip baths are very useful both during and after fasting. The ordinary full bath can be called into use for the application of the hip bath. The water should be at a temperature of between 98° and 105° F. Instead of lying in the bath, it is necessary to sit, with the knees drawn up. The water should come up to the navel. In this position the blood is drawn into the abdominal organs, and with it the toxic material to be eliminated. Sit in the hot water for ten to fifteen minutes and then subject the parts that have been in the hot water — and those parts only — to a quick, cold ablution. The cold water will drive the blood away, but, because of the law of action and reaction, it will return in greater volume. The hip bath serves to break down, de-congest and eliminate the toxic material. It is useful at all times for the cure of asthma and hay fever, but especially so when fasting. There need be no sensation of cold after the cold ablution, because the circulation is actually improved by the process.

Any person fasting for more than three to four days may feel the cold more quickly than when eating. To counteract this it may be advisable to wear more garments of a loose-fitting nature. It is certainly neither necessary nor advisable to overheat the room. Body heat can be maintained by sensible exercise and the addition of extra, light clothing. The hip and other baths are also of assistance.

WEIGHT LOSS

Abstention from food entails some loss of weight. This will vary with the individual and with the duration of the fast. The average loss of weight in a fairly stout person can be calculated at one and a half pounds per day for the first three to four days, after which it settles down to one pound per day or less. As the fast proceeds the loss of weight per day declines. In institutional treatment, of course, the loss of weight may be assisted by other means, if it is deemed necessary and safe to do so. It should be realized from the outset, however, that the slimming process is quite a good thing. What is lost is mainly in impurities which have previously clogged the system. What is gained in the after-care should be good, healthy tissue.

It should be remembered at all times that the control of fasting is a specialized technique. It demands care, knowledge and observation. The ordinary person can quite safely fast for four or five days. Over and above that period, however, some skilled supervision is required.

No one could reasonably expect to be cured of asthma and hay fever after a fast of five days, followed by a short period of after-care. A condition that has taken years of abuse and wrong living to develop, apart from the constant application of drug therapy, will not disappear overnight. Such a fast will, however, be proved of immense value in relieving the system of pent-up poisons. A feeling of lightness and renewed vitality will result from the fast.

In all probability, the fast will have to be repeated. It may, in some cases, be necessary to do the four-to-five-day fast a month for several months. The vast improvement in health and vitality and the gradual freedom from asthmatical attacks will encourage the victim of asthma and hay fever to persevere until the cure is complete. Even so, the fast will have to be followed by after-care in each case, and the general diet outlined will have to be followed.

WARNING

Long-continued fasting can induce a mental state not consistent with health. Fasting is a balanced, therapeutic procedure. It must not be confused with any religious, ideological or personal doctrines. *Fasting is a means to health — no more, no less.* While fasting has certain virtues apart from health — self-discipline, for instance — they should never be confused with the main object, which is health.

Fasting is *not* the answer to all ills, but it is the answer to a great many. In the case of asthma and hay fever controlled fasting is a great asset.

ALTERNATIVE CLEANSING

Those people who are, for one reason or another, unable or unwilling to adopt the fasting procedure, have alternative means of cleansing the system. These alternatives are, of course, slower in action than the strict fasting, but the ultimate result is essentially the same.

An *eliminating* diet can be made solely of fresh and dried fruit and raw salads. No precise limit would be made for the exact quantity of food consumed in any one day, with the exception that over-eating is always bad. The food, however, should be entirely of fruit and raw salad vegetables. Some cooked vegetables could be permitted, as, for example, potatoes in jackets, spinach, tomatoes, carrots, onions.

A typical eliminative diet would be as follows:

Breakfast:	Fruit juice
Lunch:	Grilled tomatoes on spinach
	Salad of lettuce, onion, cucumber, grated carrots
	Prunes or figs
Tea:	Fruit juice *or* thin vegetable broth
Supper:	Large raw salad (lettuce, endive, tomato, carrot, parsley, chives)
	Grapes, apples, *or* berry *or* citrus fruit.

No fats, sugars, starches or proteins are allowed in the diet, which is composed solely of the alkaline and eliminating raw and cooked fruits and vegetables.

When coming off the eliminating diet adopt the *B* menu as shown in the after-care section for one day, and then the *C* menu for another day before reverting to the general diet.

It is possible to stay on the eliminating diet for several weeks, if necessary.

The potato and onion diet is another way of eliminating, though more monotonous than the above. The potatoes should always be cooked in their skins and any water used in cooking the potatoes or onions should be taken as a drink between meals. No salt should be used in the cooking, but parsley can be added.

There are many variations of the potato and onion diet. Indeed, since the diet is exclusively of potatoes and onions some variation in order should be welcomed. The following is merely a specimen which can be altered as desired, so long as no addition is made to the potatoes and onions other than that of chopped parsley.

Breakfast:	Thick potato broth
Lunch:	Baked potatoes
	Steamed onions
Tea:	Potato and onion broth with chopped parsley
Supper:	Steamed potatoes
	Boiled onions

The potato and onion diet can be kept up for two to three weeks. When breaking the diet adopt menu *A* for the first three days, menu *B* for two more days, then menu *C* for two days, and then change over to the general diet.

It must be emphasized that fasting is infinitely superior to either of the above, so far as elimination of toxic products is concerned. However, the above can be carried out at home while continuing one's normal daily work. This factor is of interest and advantage to those who are unable to free themselves of occupational demands while attempting to cure asthma or hay fever.

8.
The After-care Period

Just as important as fasting is the period of after-care following the fast. It is important for two reasons. The first is that it is essential to avoid any gastric distress, arising from the consumption of wrong food at a time when the digestive organs have been rested and are unprepared. The second reason is that the eliminatory process does not suddenly end with breaking the fast. By the ingestion of correct food gastric distress is avoided and elimination proceeds — albeit more slowly. A very heavy meal, for instance, after fasting would be a great shock to the system. It would produce gastric discomfort and great disruption of the eliminatory process created by fasting. Breaking the fast, therefore, requires some care.

Whether the fasting period has lasted three or ten days it is the best plan to have fruit only on the first day following the fast. The breakfast would be of fruit juice only, with fruit at lunch, fruit juice at tea-time and fruit again in the evening. If the fast has been carried out for a period longer than five days the same procedure should be adopted for at least two days after the fast. Suitable fruit would be apples, oranges, grapes, grapefruit, dates, prunes, figs and raisins. Small amounts of fruit would be taken on the first day. When the fast has been conducted for ten to fourteen days, at least three days on fruit alone would be advised.

The fruit meals would be gradually extended to include, first of all, salads, and later cooked vegetables — gradually reverting to the normal diet as outlined in Chapter 6. It will be appreciated that the longer the fast has been the more after-care is required.

To obtain the very best results from the fast it is, in fact, advisable to follow it up by an eliminative diet. This would mean having fruit only for the first seven days and then fruit and raw salads for another seven days. The following chart will be found a useful guide:

AFTER-CARE FOR FASTS FROM THREE TO FIVE DAYS

First day of fast
(A)   *Breakfast*:   Fruit juice
      Lunch: Apple, grapes *or* grapefruit
                          6 dates
      Tea: Fruit juice
      Supper: 2 apples, prunes *or* figs, orange
Second day
      Repeat first day
Third day
(B)   *Breakfast*:   Fruit juice *or* Muesli
      Lunch: Small raw salad
                          Baked apple and few dates
                          Orange *or* grapefruit *or* berry fruit
      Tea: Fruit juice
      Supper: Baked potato. Raw salad. Prunes *or* figs with dates
                          or raisins

Fourth day

(C)   *Breakfast*: Fruit juice or Muesli *or* stewed prunes with little
                   cereal

        Lunch: Poached egg *or* mushrooms on spinach with
                   Steamed potatoes
                   Grilled tomatoes
                   Carrots
                   Baked apple

        Tea: Weak tea *or* fruit juice

        Supper: Raw salad
                   Biscuits and butter and little cheese
                   Apple and grapes *or* baked banana and dates

AFTER-CARE FOR FASTS FROM FIVE TO TEN DAYS

First day:	Same as (*A*).
Second day:	Same as (*A*)
Third day:	Same as (*A*).
Fourth day:	Same as (*A*).
Fifth day:	Same as (*B*).
Sixth day:	Same as (*B*).
Seventh day:	Same as (*C*).

For fasts of ten days or over, allow at least seven days
on the *A* type fruit menu, followed by four to five days on
the *B* and two days on the *C* before coming on to the
normal food reform diet regime.

It is of the utmost importance to adhere rigidly to the
correct after-care period before embarking upon the more
liberal general diet. By doing so, the full benefit of the fast
will be assured, elimination will continue and gastric
discomfort be avoided. Quite a lot depends upon the
season of the year as to what fruit and vegetables are
available, but sufficient fruit and salad materials are
normally to be obtained all the year round, and there is no
valid reason why good bottled (unsweetened) fruit should
not be used.

9.
Water Treatments

The hip bath and enema in the treatment of asthma and hay fever have already been discussed. These are just two of the many hydropathic measures that can be carried out in the home. A simple gravity douche will give an adequate enema.

One of the simplest water treatments is the daily *cold friction rub*. All that is required is a coarse towel and cold water. Dip the towel into cold water and lightly wring it out. Start from the feet, working upwards, and scrub every part of the body with the wet towel. The cold friction should be done quite vigorously, and the final result should show a glowing skin. It may be advisable for beginners to stand with the feet in a bowl of warm water for the first few times. The cold friction rub tones and hardens the skin, prevents chills and bronchitis and improves the circulation and nervous system.

BATHS

The rising and falling bath is very easy to carry out at home. The ordinary bath is filled with water at a temperature of between 95° and 100° F. The patient lies in this water, then the hot tap is turned on and the water is allowed to rise to between 108° and 100° F. Sweating will probably result at this stage and should be maintained for five to six minutes before the temperature is lowered by the addition of cold water, to 75° and 85° F.

The object of this bath, like all water treatments, is to dissolve, eliminate and strengthen. It dissolves poisons into a condition where they can be freely eliminated, assists elimination and strengthens the body. Unlike the hip bath, the rising and falling bath should not be taken by cases complicated by heart trouble without expert advice.

The relaxing bath is of special benefit to asthma and hay fever subjects in that it is particularly helpful to the nervous system. The temperature of the bath should be kept at about 90° to 93°. F. for as long as forty to sixty minutes. This temperature ensures a pleasant feeling of relaxation, and it is advisable to stay in the water for at least forty minutes to produce the relaxation of nervous tension that is desired. It will often be found that the addition of a little pine.oil will make it more effective in asthma cases. It can, normally, be quite safely taken in all cases, including those with heart trouble, and will be found very beneficial.

The Epsom salt bath can quite easily be applied at home. Allow 1 to 1½ lb of the commercial Epsom salts for each bath. Epsom salt neutralizes the acid waste products of the body and assists the elimination of such acids. It is particularly useful for all cases of asthma and hay fever because of its eliminating effects. The hot water should not be more than 105° F., and it is not desirable to stay in the salt bath for more than ten minutes. Over this period there is a danger of palpitation and faintness, especially in elderly people.

It is not advisable to take this bath while fasting, except under supervision, and it is not suitable for heart cases. The salt bath is, however, a very useful addition to home treatment, provided that sensible precautions are observed and the time limit is not exceeded. It is *very necessary to cool down* with a cold splash or shower after the salt bath (as after any hot bath) and to have at least an hour's rest after the treatment. The salt bath should not be taken more than twice in a week.

The hot foot bath is extremely useful at a time when an attack of asthma may be pending. Sit with the feet in a bowl of water as hot as can comfortably be borne. This will draw the blood from the upper parts of the body and reduce the congestion in that area. The same treatment for the hands will often be found effective.

'STEAMING'

Steaming of the nose, throat and chest frequently alleviates the irritated condition of the mucous lining of the air passages and facilitates the expulsion of mucus. The steam heat penetrates the air-passages more effectively than most forms of heat. While a steam kettle is a useful addition for the home treatment of asthma and hay fever, it is not essential. The ordinary domestic kettle can be made to serve the same purpose.

The kettle should be about two-thirds full of water and a steady jet of steam maintained. The steam must be directed on the nose, throat and chest for at least ten to fifteen minutes, and the process concluded by cold water applications to the steamed parts. The addition of a little pine oil to the water used for steaming is advised. It is, of course, possible to steam the head and shoulder regions by bending over a bowl of very hot water while a piece of sheeting covers the head and shoulders and encloses the bowl. This is a very effective method, but it does entail a cramped position which is avoided by the use of a kettle.

PACKS AND COMPRESSES

Packs and compresses are simple hydropathic measures which can be usefully employed in the treatment of asthma or hay fever. Cold compresses applied to the back of the neck will help reduce tension and congestion in the head and neck. Two or three large handkerchiefs or a small handtowel or piece of sheeting will serve as a compress. These should be repeated till sufficient relief is found.

For general purposes the three-quarter body pack is the one best advised in the treatment of asthma or hay fever. It should be said here, however, that packs are not advisable when fasting or if a warm reaction is not quickly obtained. Fasting entails some loss of body heat, and for this reason cold packs should be avoided. The cold pack depends upon moist warmth for its efficacy and, therefore, if a warm reaction is not obtained within a few minutes it is unwise to continue. By placing hot water bottles in the bed it is possible to ensure a warm reaction.

All that is required for the pack is an unbleached cotton sheet, a thick blanket and a piece of rubber sheeting to protect the mattress. Dip the sheet into a bowl of cold water, and then wring out all the superfluous water, leaving the sheet quite wet. Draw the coverings from the bed and place the rubber sheeting under the bottom sheet to protect the mattress. On the bottom sheet lay the blanket so that the sides overlap the bed. On the blanket place the wet sheet in such a way that, when the patient lies on it, the wet sheet covers the entire body from shoulders down, leaving only the arms and head free. The patient lies on the sheet in the manner described, and the sheet is immediately pulled over and secured with safety pins. The blanket is then drawn over and pinned, and the normal bed covering is then placed over the patient. Hot water bottles, if necessary, are placed in the bed, and the patient is allowed to remain in the pack for two to three hours.

On emerging from the pack he or she is advised to have a cold friction rub or a warm bath followed by a cold shower.

The pack is applied mainly because it increases skin activity and we have learnt that efficient functioning of the skin is essential to elimination. The cold pack achieves the cardinal tasks of all water treatments, *i.e.*, it serves to dissolve, eliminate and strengthen. The cold pack draws the blood to the superficial tissues, thus relieving inner congestion; the blood contained in the superficial tissues induces a moist warmth which dissolves acids circulating in the blood and relaxes the skin and the minute pores and blood-vessels, permitting effete matter to escape from the body into the sheet.

Apart from the promotion of elimination, however, the pack has a soothing effect upon the nerves and serves to strengthen and tone both the skin and the nervous system. But, as we have already stressed, the success of the pack depends upon the warm reaction and the ensuing moist warmth. If its application is successful the pack will be found most valuable in the treatment of both asthma and hay fever.

Water treatments are inexpensive yet effective methods of assisting the cure of asthma and hay fever. There is no reason, providing that common sense is used, why they should not be successfully employed in the home treatment of both diseases under discussion.

10.
Physiotherapy

From what has been previously said it will be fully appreciated that all forms of movement must be adopted to ensure: firstly, a good supply of oxygen; secondly, unrestricted movement of blood and interchange of oxygen and carbon dioxide; thirdly, the elimination of carbon dioxide and all other waste products. Any movement that assists or accelerates one or all of the above helps to effect the cure of asthmatical conditions.

In both asthma and hay fever rigidity of the thorax and cervical spine is often shown. The shoulders are particularly affected, and every effort should be made to ensure mobility in the upper chest. Contraction of the ribs and inter-costal muscles arises in all asthmatical conditions. It is of the utmost importance to gain the maximum amount of freedom of motion in the ribs and underlying tissues. So far only the local stiffness and contraction that are produced largely by the attacks of asthma or hay fever have been mentioned. By the aid of exercises, massage and manipulation, both the whole system and the localized regions of the body gain greater mobility, an easier flow of the blood-stream and a more efficient interchange of chemical products.

DEEP BREATHING

First and foremost comes the need for the full use of the lungs and a maximum supply of oxygen and output of carbon dioxide. Deep-breathing exercises at the open window for at least ten minutes night and morning are essential. While there are many variations of deep-breathing exercises, it is generally agreed that it is advisable to breathe in and out through the nose. Breathing through the nose makes use of the natural filtering mechanism of the air-passages.

· The deep breathing should be performed either out-doors or at the open window, irrespective of the weather. One method is to inhale slowly and deeply, at the same time raising the shoulders as high as possible. When exhaling, let the shoulders drop with a jerk. Another method is to stand erect with the arms at the sides. Inhale deeply, at the same time raising the arms as high as possible over the head. When the arms are outstretched over the head, clasp and unclasp the hands before exhaling. A deep expiration always encourages a deep inspiration; thus, by the institution of deep-breathing exercises the normal breathing is made deeper. Exhaling should take about twice the time of inhaling, to ensure the best results.

Efficient oxygenation of the blood-stream will be of considerable benefit to the system and, indeed, is an absolute necessity.

EXERCISE AND RELAXATION

Deep-breathing exercises, however, are not sufficient in themselves. All forms of exercise are desirable — walking, arm and leg exercises, trunk and abdominal exercises, etc. Included among the exercises are the various relaxing positions and correct posture. The need for mental and physical relaxation is very great in both asthma and hay fever.

To induce relaxation lie flat on the bed or floor and let the arms and legs go absolutely limp, keeping the mind as blank as possible. There should be no conscious effort to relax, and an absence of mental and physical effort should be aimed at. Another way of relaxing is to lie flat on the floor with the legs at right angles resting on the wall. It is necessary to bend the knees every few minutes, putting them back in the upright position against the wall. The buttocks should be as near as possible to the base of the wall when in this relaxing position.

Yawning, laughing and stretching are largely involuntary movements which exert a beneficial effect upon the system. All the movements instituted by laughter, for instance, have an effect upon the lungs, diaphragm and abdominal viscera.

Correct posture is a great advantage. Insofar as is possible a correct posture should be maintained at all times. When sitting, care must be taken to avoid pressure effects and cramping of the abdominal organs. The head should not be inclined so far forward that tension in the cervical region is bound to arise, nor should the chest be cramped by bending. The slumping attitude so often adopted is detrimental to the lungs. Correct posture can be simply described as *head up, chin in, chest up and out (but not puffed out), shoulders high, abdomen in, legs straight and feet forward so that the body inclines lightly forward.*

MASSAGE

Massage possesses all the attributes of water treatment in that, by its adoption, it is possible to break down toxins, ensure the elimination of effete matter and strengthen the body. All the healing powers of the body are assisted by massage.

Massage can have a soothing or stimulating effect, according to what is desired and necessary for the patient.

Mobility can be restored to contracted and tense tissues and joints, and the blood and lymphatic systems can be regulated. By stimulating the chemical processes of the body and ensuring the drainage of waste matter, massage exerts a beneficial effect upon the entire organism. It tones the nervous system and builds healthy tissue.

It is, however, much for its local effects that massage is employed in asthma and hay fever. By its employment a great deal of relief can be gained in all cases of the diseases. Tension and contraction in the whole thoracic region can be alleviated and the ribs and underlying muscles made more mobile. This allows greater freedom for the lungs to expand, and a more efficient interchange of oxygen and carbon dioxide thereby results. The action of the heart, too, is assisted by massage.

MANIPULATION

Manipulation covers a large field and very often includes massage, osteopathy and chiropractic. Manipulation is more deep-reaching than massage, and adjustment of osseous and tissue lesions, impossible by massage movements only, calls for some manipulative treatment. In asthma and hay fever, where maladjustment can arise from asthmatical attacks, manipulation is widely indicated.

As has been previously observed, the severity of the asthmatical paroxysms causes contraction and tension in the thoracic and cervical regions. If unattended, these contractions become a permanent feature and induce further attacks by the lack of mobility and tension in the very region where freedom of movement is essential to the functioning of the lungs. Any impediment of free expansion of the lungs or to the expectoration of mucus helps to create asthmatical attacks. Neuro-muscular tension and contraction of tissues, plus faulty drainage and lack of oxygen, play a large part in the etiology of asthma and hay fever.

Manipulation, apart from giving almost immediate relief, provides a satisfactory means of assisting the cure of

asthma and hay fever. It is able to exert a beneficial
influence on the intimate nerve connections between the
stomach and the lungs — a vital factor in the treatment of
asthmatical conditions. With manipulative treatment
increased mobility is found, a free flow of the chemical
products of the body is assured and resistance to disease is
increased. Only manipulation can provide the adjustment
of bony lesions that are so frequently found in asthma and
hay fever.

Massage and manipulation, of course, cannot be self-
applied. It will, however, be proved advantageous to take a
course of manipulative treatment when attempting to cure
asthma or hay fever.

SUNLIGHT TREATMENT

Most allergic conditions, including asthma and hay fever,
respond to sunlight treatment. Sunlight kills bacteria, helps
to regulate the blood-pressure, increases metabolism and
respiration, stimulates the circulation and exerts a beneficial influence on the chemical secretions of the body. It is,
of course, well known that the sun's rays exert a powerful
effect on the formation of vitamin D.

The effect of sunlight on the skin is to cause erythema.
This is the redness of the skin always associated with
sun-bathing. The extent to which it takes places varies with
the pigmentation of the individual. Sunlight brings the
blood into the superficial tissues and creates warmth. Most
of the good effects of sunlight are produced by the
ultra-violet rays, and when the skin is warm the ultra-violet
rays are able to penetrate deeper into the tissues and
produce more valuable tonic effects.

The creation of ultra-violet rays by artificial means has
undoubtedly been a boon to suffering mankind. Use is
made of the sun's rays independent of the weather. The
same factors that produce the beneficial effect from
normal sunlight are reproduced in thousands of clinics and
private office practices. Ultra-violet ray treatment, given
after or during the time when the body is warm from

massage or heat treatment, is extremely helpful to the cure of asthma and hay fever. Ultra-violet treatment is often given in conjunction with massage or manipulation.

Apart from any treatment by ultra-violet irradiation, every effort should be made to make as much use as possible of the natural sunlight. Sunbathing can be indulged in to a great degree, though the initial stages require some care. Exposure should begin with a few moments only, especially if the person is fair. A good plan is to spend a few minutes in the sun, followed by half an hour in the shade, then a few more moments in the sun. Gradually increase the exposure to the sun as the days progress. Always have a cold shower after a sunbath so as to close the pores and prevent any chill. Even moving from sun to shade sets up a form of skin gymnastics which is beneficial to the skin action and the nervous system.

Air-bathing, which can be practised in the privacy of the bedroom, independent of the weather, should be a daily habit. All exercises are best carried out in the nude. Air-bathing tones and strengthens both the skin function and the nervous system. The daily air-bath will harden the skin, dispel any tendency to chills and draughts, and pave the way for safe sunbathing.

It must be remembered at all times that the sun, air and water are three of nature's most efficacious remedies.

II.
Conclusion

Herbal treatment is often recommended in the treatment of asthma and hay fever. It is most certainly of great value. We must, however, warn against the habit of relying on this or that remedy alone. It would be the height of folly to assume that, provided a genuine herbal remedy was taken, it would be unnecessary to restrict the diet or to correct any other fault contributing to the asthmatical state. Yet such ideas are often held.

No one thing will ever cure asthma; it may palliate the condition, but the only successful remedy is that which recognizes all the factors at work in the etiology of asthma and hay fever and seeks, as far as possible, to eliminate all the detrimental factors involved.

The body must be treated as a whole, and it is impossible, owing to the inter-dependence between one organ and another, to separate the body into units and treat just one of them.

The human organism can best be described as a State which is divided into self-governing provinces, each with its own measure of independence, but all dependent upon one another and subject to the ultimate authority of the State. In this case the brain is the State, the various organs and systems the provinces. And, for efficiency and economy, all the provinces of the body are dependent upon the body-politic for harmonious function. Discord (disease) in any one organ or system has repercussions throughout the entire organism.

It is for this reason, as much as any other, that a warning is given regarding the adoption of pills and potions. Such remedies, herbal and otherwise, may be excellent in themselves. If, however, as is often the case, they are primarily intended for the relief, palliation or cure of symptoms — and not the disease as a whole — it is best to be aware of the fact. Such awareness will lessen the tendency to rely solely on medication.

This point is stressed so as to explain the necessity for an all-round effort to cure the disease and to avoid falling into the trap of assuming that medication alone, no matter how non-poisonous, will perform the miracle of curing asthma or hay fever.

SMOKING

Take the case of tobacco. A pipe or cigarette is often

indulged in because it is presumed, at the time, to steady
the nerves. Tobacco, of course, is an irritant poison which
depresses the nervous system, raises the blood-pressure, has
a debilitating effect upon the heart and is a severe
irritation to the delicate mucous membrane lining the
air-passages. The smoker's cough results from irritation of
tissue and nerve-endings. In the case of asthma and hay
fever, where irritation of the air-passage already exists, the
smoking habit is decidedly harmful.

Any chemical or mechanical irritant that is known to
have an adverse effect upon the asthmatical stage must be
avoided it it is at all possible. It is not always an easy
matter to change from a locality, known to be detrimental,
to another which is recognized as beneficial. It should,
however, be possible to do something about the occupational irritants that aggravate asthma. It should, too, not
be difficult to avoid crowded and ill-ventilated buildings
such as cinemas and concert halls.

WORRY

Worry, fear, anger and all intense emotional outbursts
create their own chemical products, most of which are
harmful to the system. Keeping in mind the nervous
characteristics of asthma or hay fever, every effort should
be made to ensure a calm and philosophical attitude.
Anger, fear and worry can have such drastic effects upon
the digestion that the wise person will always take heed of
the natural instinct in such conditions and avoid eating.

Over-work and fatigue produce poisons no less than the
habit of taking drugs. To eat when tired is to depress the
system further, tax the digestion and create a condition
favourable for an asthmatical attack. Stimulating a tired
body or brain with tea, coffee, or drugs is a grave mistake
which is very prevalent. It uses up reserves of nervous
energy, and as in all cases, over-stimulation produces
ultimate depression.

Few people can truthfully say that it is impossible to
overcome all the difficulties in the way of exercising,

obtaining fresh air and sunlight, carrying out the water treatments, adhering to the correct diet or adopting moderation in all things. It is only by overcoming the difficulties that asthma and hay fever can be cured. The measure of such determination to overcome obstacles is the measure of the will to be cured.

Nature Cure is not expensive. Any additional expense that may arise from the cost of the diet (though no additional cost is actually necessary) is more than offset by the saving in drugs and by the additional earning capacity that freedom from asthmatical attacks brings. Count the saving in human happiness, health and contentment, and the triumph of natural methods becomes obvious.

Nature Cure is the common-sense method of curing all diseases, and asthma and hay fever are curable.

Have you read these best selling ABOUT books?

ABOUT GINSENG

This book tells how ginseng has been used as a panacea for thousands of years in the East, describes its natural habitat and its cultivation throughout the world, and gives scientific evidence of its properties — especially its effect on the ageing process. The author reviews the different forms available and gives advice on how best to take it.

ABOUT VITAMINS

In this age of processed foods it is becoming increasingly more important to ensure that our diets provide us with an adequate supply of vitamins for the maintenance of good health. This book, an introduction to the subject of vitamins, clears away any misunderstandings that might exist, and tells the fascinating story of man's discovery of nature's keys to radiant health.

ABOUT RAW JUICES

The juices of fresh fruit and vegetables play a vital part in restoring and maintaining optimum health, and this book shows you how to select, prepare and use such life-giving and delicious drinks both for fortification against disease and for the specific treatment of certain ailments.

ABOUT GARLIC

Gives the historical background to this amazing herb, and shows how its miraculous healing powers can protect your health and assist the cure of many and varied complaints. The book also contains hints on the use of garlic in the kitchen, and recipes are included for garlic flavoured dishes.